I Hope You
Know How
Much I
Love You!

and Other Advice
for a Happier Life

I Hope You Know How Much I Love You!

and Other Advice
for a Happier Life

John Bytheway

Salt Lake City, Utah

Illustrations by Bryan Beach; © 2011 Deseret Book Company

© 2011 John Bytheway

Visit us at DeseretBook.com

Library of Congress Cataloging-in-Publication Data
Bytheway, John (John Glenn), 1962–
  I hope you know how much I love you and other advice for a happier life / John Bytheway.
     pages cm
  Includes bibliographical references.
  ISBN 978-1-60641-947-2 (hardbound : alk. paper)
  1. Christian life—Mormon authors. 2. Conduct of life. I. Title.
  BX8656.B885 2011
  248.4'89332—dc22   2010048975

Printed in Mexico
R.R. Donnelley, Reynosa, Mexico

10   9   8   7   6   5   4   3   2   1

Contents

Preface vii

Comparing, Competing,
    and Being Content 1

The Greatest Success Formula 11

I Think I'll Be Delightful Today 17

Two, Four, Six, Eight, Who
    Do We Appreciate? 23

Hope Smiling Brightly before Us 30

Why Me? Why This? Why Now? 37

Perspective 43

Notes 53

Preface

Mom taught me simple things when I was little. Do your best. Be good. Be nice. Say "thank you." And don't worry, everything will be all right.

Then I got older, and my life got a lot more complicated—I got married, I got a mortgage, I got a job. I had children with their own challenges. The simple answers, however, remained just as true. For me, "do your best" became *be content*. "Be good" became *keep the Spirit*. "Be nice" evolved into *choose happiness even when things are hard*. "Say thank you" was restated as *have an attitude of gratitude*. And "Don't worry" grew into a message about *hope* and an *eternal perspective*. In this little book we'll go through each of these simple ideas again. Yes, they're simple, but that doesn't mean they're obsolete or outdated or only for kids. Because some things are simple, and some things are simply true.

Comparing, Competing, and Being Content

SOME OF THE GREATEST life lessons I know have come from the women in my life. And I am sure it is the same for many of you. The women who have been there for us, supported us, and buoyed us up know about life and its hardships and how we can make it through with graciousness and hope.

I remember hearing President Hinckley's daughters talk about their mother at a women's event I attended. When they showed Marjorie Pay Hinckley's photo on the screen, we could all see a life of goodness reflected in her countenance. We could see the wisdom of years written in her face, along with a twinkle in her eye that revealed her delightful sense of humor. She spoke to women as only another woman could, and her words were backed by experience and endorsed with testimony. She said:

> We women have a lot to learn about simplifying our lives. We have to decide what is important and then move along at a pace that is comfortable for us. We have to develop the maturity to stop trying to prove something. We have to learn to be content with what we are.[1]
>
> —Marjorie Pay Hinckley

Contentment is a difficult commodity to obtain in a world that is busily trying to convince us that we must have it all, we must have it all of the time, and we must look gorgeous, sophisticated, and brilliant while having it. You can jump on that treadmill if you want, but you'll never be able to keep pace with the mythical image of the superwoman the advertising agencies have created. Instead, within the gospel, we are counseled to focus on finding contentment. The Apostle Paul shared what he had discovered in these words: "For I have learned, in whatsoever state I am, therewith to be content" (Philippians 4:11).

Being content allows you to be yourself. It means you can stop comparing and competing with the other people around you. I'm convinced that contentment is a spiritual gift, while competition is a manmade distraction from what is really important. Sister Hinckley found that the moment she quit competing was the moment she felt happiest:

> Within the gospel we are counseled to focus on finding contentment.

Fifty was my favorite age. It takes about that long to learn to quit competing—to be yourself and settle down to living. It is the age I would like to be through all eternity![2]

—Marjorie Pay Hinckley

Saying "yes" to contentment and "no" to competition means we are not threatened by the accomplishments of others. Patricia Holland once taught:

> There seems to be an increase in our competitiveness and a decrease in our generosity with one another.
>
> Those who have the time and energy to can their fruit and vegetables develop a great skill that will serve them well in time of need—and in our uncertain economic times, that could be almost any day of the week. But they shouldn't look down their noses at those who buy their peaches, or who don't like zucchini in any of the thirty-five ways there are to disguise it, or who have simply made a conscious choice to use their time and energy in some other purposeful way.
>
> And where am I in all of this? For three-fourths of my life I was threatened to the core because I hated to sew. Now I *can* sew; if absolutely forced to, I *will* sew—but I hate it. Imagine my burden over the last twenty-five or thirty years, faking it in Relief Society sessions and trying to smile when six little girls walk into church all pinafored and laced and ribboned and petticoated—identical, hand

sewn—all trooping ahead of their mother, who has the same immaculate outfit. Competitive? I wanted to tear their pleats out.

I don't necessarily consider it virtuous, lovely, or of good report, or praiseworthy—but I'm honest in my antipathy toward sewing. If even one sister out there is weeping tears of relief, then I consider my public shame at least a partial blow against stereotyping. I have grown up a little since those days in at least two ways— I now genuinely admire a mother who can do that for her children, and I have ceased feeling guilty that sewing is not particularly rewarding to me. We simply cannot call ourselves Christian and continue to judge one another—or ourselves—so harshly.[3]

—Patricia Terry Holland

We simply cannot call ourselves Christian and continue to judge one another—or ourselves— so harshly.
—Patricia Terry Holland

Ta-da!

When Alma returned from his mission, he happened to run into his former companions whom he hadn't seen in years. Alma learned of their tremendous successes while they were apart, and what was his response? *Wow, you guys did really well. Now I'm depressed.* Did Alma look at his friends as competitors or rivals? No. Alma was thrilled with the success of others:

> But I do not joy in my own success alone, but my joy is more full because of the success of my brethren. . . . Now, when I think of the success of these my brethren my soul is carried away, even to the separation of it from the body, as it were, so great is my joy (Alma 29:14, 16).

We are brothers and sisters. We are in this together. We are not competing against each other, but against evil. And yes, as we confront the busyness of life, and the endless to-do lists, inevitably, some things will be left undone. And you know what? That's okay. A phrase I learned once at a women's conference about choosing to let some things go undone is called "selective neglect." As Sister Hinckley has said:

> Choose carefully each day that which you will do and that which you will not do, and the Lord will bless you to accomplish the important things that have eternal consequences. At my age, I've edited the scripture just a little: "For it is not requisite that a woman should hobble faster than she has strength."[4]
>
> —Marjorie Pay Hinckley

The bottom line is, we simply cannot do it all. And that's okay. The challenge is, given all we have to do, to spend our time on the best things. This process of choosing how to spend our time is where the gospel becomes immensely practical. The gospel

We are in this together. We are not competing against each other, but against evil.

helps us see what is really important and what isn't. It clears the mists of darkness and lets us see into eternity.

I've heard it said that cleaning the house while the children are growing is like shoveling snow when the clouds are still snowing. One step forward, two steps back, right? In my home, we have two cleaners and six messers. When you've grown up hearing that "cleanliness is next to godliness," it's a 24/7 challenge to meet that ideal. In our home, cleanliness is next to impossible. What do you do, when you have to choose between being a mom or a maid? My wife discovered this poem and shared it with me:

Excuse This House

*Some homes try to hide the fact that children
  shelter there.*
*Ours boasts of it quite openly, the signs are
  everywhere!*
*For smears are on the windows, little smudges
  on the door.*
*I should apologize, I guess, for toys strewn on the
  floor.*
*But I sat down with the children and we played
  and laughed and read;*

*And if the doorbell doesn't shine, their eyes will
    shine instead.
For when at times I'm forced to choose the one
    job or the other,
I want to be a homemaker—but first I'll be a
    mother.*[5]

So what do we do? We do the best we can. All
you can do, is all you can do.

Therefore, dearly beloved [sisters], let us
cheerfully do all things that lie in our power; and
then may we stand still, with the utmost assur-
ance, to see the sal-   vation of God,
and for his arm to
be revealed (D&C
123:17).

When you do
the best you can,
you can be at peace,
and with the Lord's
spirit, you can feel
content.

When you do the best you can, you can be at peace, and with the Lord's spirit, you can feel content.

The Greatest Success Formula

A T ANOTHER WOMEN'S EVENT I attended, I was mesmerized by the outcome of an experiment conducted by Wendy Watson Nelson. For two weeks, she asked women to do a simple exercise, and the results were stunning. Here's what the women who participated in the experiment reported:

- An increased desire to de-junk their physical environments
- A greatly reduced desire to watch TV
- An increased desire to reach out to others and to follow through on commitments
- An increased ability to be kinder, gentler, and more patient

- An increased desire to take care of their bodies by living the Lord's law of health more fully
- An increased ability to see how they could have handled situations better
- An increased mental focus
- An increased ability and desire to really study and learn
- Old habits of backbiting, gossiping, and cynicalness falling away
- A dramatic increase in their physical energy, because energy-draining negative emotions were gone
- An unbelievable reduction in stress
- Profound changes in their conversations with others

By the time she finished the list, I was fit to be tied. What in the world did they do? Who wouldn't want all of these things? Who wouldn't pay a "personal success coach" if they could get these results? So, along with all of the other people in the audience, I was on the edge of my chair, waiting for the profound particulars of the experiment. And what I

heard was so simple, so doable, and so obvious. The experiment was something I should have known all along:

> For five days in their morning prayers, they were to pray with concerted effort for the Holy Ghost to be with them that day. Then, throughout the day, as they encountered any difficult, tempting or trying situation, they were to pray for and really picture the Spirit being right there with them.[6]
>
> —Wendy Watson Nelson

That was it. Strive to have the Spirit to be with you and really focus on the reality of that divine companionship in times of stress. It dawned on me, that for all the self-help books out there, for all the experts in goal-setting and achievement,

Strive to have the Spirit to be with you and really focus on the reality of that divine companionship in times of stress.

for all the infomercials and seminars, that what we really need we are already offered every Sunday. The greatest success formula ever devised is repeated weekly by sixteen-year-old boys as they say:

> . . . and witness unto thee, O God, the Eternal Father, that they are willing to take upon them the name of thy Son, and always remember him, and keep his commandments which he hath given them, that they may always have his Spirit to be with them (Moroni 4:3).

This was never a hidden formula. This was something the Lord had given us all along. We are blessed with the companionship of a member of the Godhead. Grace is defined as the Lord's enabling power, and with the power of his grace, not only can we find contentment, but we can be at peace, and we can be kind and loving and patient beyond our natural abilities because we can "always have his Spirit to be with [us]."

The Apostle Paul described the armor of God in Ephesians 6. The first five items he mentions are

> The Spirit isn't just there to make you feel nice while the world is beating you up. The Spirit is an infusion of enabling power and allows you to push back against the world.

defensive armor, but that last item is a weapon—the "sword of the Spirit." Jeffrey R. Holland explained that this sword allows us to actually "do battle" with the world. The Spirit isn't just there to make you feel nice while the world is beating you up. The Spirit is an infusion of enabling power and allows you to push back against the world.[7]

Perhaps this is why Melvin J. Ballard said, "The one thing that would make for the safety of every man and woman would be to appear at the sacrament table every Sabbath day. . . . The road to the sacrament table is the path of safety for Latter-day Saints."[8]

I Think I'll Be Delightful Today

IMET A WOMAN FULL OF grace on a cruise ship. We were traveling with a small LDS tour, and we got to know everyone in our group. Her name was Donna, and whenever she had the opportunity to speak, she talked about how much she just *loved* being with her husband. I thought it was very sweet at first, but after a while, after repeatedly hearing her express about how much she just LOVED to travel with Ken, her husband, I, along with probably a few other men, started to get a bit curious.

What is it about this guy? we thought. Is he really that fun to be with, or is he just trying to live up to his wife's expectations? So I decided to hang out with Ken. And I found out that Donna was right. Ken was pretty fun to be with. But here's the question—was he that way on his own, or because his wife described him that way? And the answer is— "Who cares!" If you have a husband who is delightful to be with, who cares why!

I started to examine my own behavior on the cruise, and I began to wonder if I was a delightful travel companion, or if I let myself get stressed when we were late getting back, or late leaving the room to meet the others, or late with our luggage, and so on. Anyway, I decided then and there that I was going to try to be more like Ken.

Now, as I approach the bathroom mirror each morning, I try to say to myself, "I think I'll be delightful." I don't know what will happen today, but I can choose to respond delightfully to anything that

I don't know what will happen today, but I can choose to respond delightfully to anything that does happen, good or bad.

does happen, good or bad. I learned that idea from Donna and Ken. My wife and I have discussed this at length, and it has become a perpetual goal in our marriage. I want my wife to enjoy being with me, and she wants me to enjoy being with her.

I have often assembled a notebook with a dozen or so goals I had for the year, and at the end of each month I would check my progress. After that cruise, one of my monthly goals became to "be delightful." I decided to let my wife, Kim, determine if I achieved it or not. That's pressure. But it's positive pressure.

Watch for the word "delightful" in the following paragraph from Sister Marjorie Pay Hinckley:

> I know it is hard for you young mothers to believe that almost before you can turn around the children will be gone and you will be alone with your husband. You had better be sure you are developing the kind of love and friendship that will be delightful and enduring. Let the children learn from your attitude that he is important. Encourage him. Be kind. It is a rough world, and

I will be delightful today.

he, like everyone else, is fighting to survive. Be cheerful. Don't be a whiner.[9]

—Marjorie Pay Hinckley

The actress Katharine Hepburn made a bittersweet observation: "If you want to sacrifice the admiration of many men for the criticism of one, go ahead, get married."[10] There's not much "sweet" in that, so perhaps it's just a bitter observation. Criticism is bitter. Is that what we hope for in marriage? To have an "in-house" criticizer? Someone to constantly remind us of how we fall short? Why would anyone want that? Why would anyone want to come home to that?

Wendy Watson Nelson once joked to a group of women about criticism. "It's not nagging," she said, "It's continuous encouragement." However, Wendy knew that what may be intended as "continuous encouragement" to one person may feel like "perpetual dissatisfaction" to another.

As Sister Hinckley said, it is a rough world. And everyone is fighting to survive. A verse of scripture that may give us insight into the right amount of criticism seems appropriate here:

> Therefore, strengthen your brethren [and your sisters] in all your conversation, in all your prayers, in all your exhortations, and in all your doings (D&C 108:7).

The word "all" appears four times in that verse. Now I haven't done third grade math in a while, but how high a percentage is "all"?

Difficult things happen to all of us. Sometimes things are not hunky-dory. But every one of us can think of people we know who have endured worse than we have and who have remained delightful through it all. We can all think of people we know who never say unkind things about others. And if they can do it, then through the enabling power of Christ, so can we.

Every one of us knows people who have endured worse than we have and who have remained delightful through it all. If they can do it, then through the enabling power of Christ, so can we.

Two, Four, Six, Eight, Who Do We Appreciate?

A WONDERFUL QUESTION TO ask oneself is, "What is it like to be married to me?" If I were married to me, would I be happy? Would I love being around me? Am I fun to be with?

My wife and I attended a BYU Campus Education Week seminar on marriage taught by Dr. Charles Beckert. He wrote three words on the blackboard, which we've never forgotten:

Appreciate / Expect / Demand

He mentioned that when we are first married, we appreciate everything. "Thanks for making dinner, thanks for putting away the dishes, thanks for cleaning the windshield, thanks, thanks, thanks!"

> If I were married to me, would I be happy? Would I love being around me? Am I fun to be with?

However, over time, we come to *expect* behavior that initially we appreciated. *You've always done this before, so you should keep doing it now*, we think.

Then, it gets worse. What we've come to expect, we begin to demand. "Where's my dinner?" "Why don't I have any clean socks this morning?" "You were supposed to put gas in my car."

Appreciate, expect, or demand? We got the message. And in that workshop, my wife and I decided to try to stay on "appreciate," and never move to "expect."

I remember one morning when the alarm clock interrupted my sleep, and I stumbled through the darkness to the bathroom. I had to get up long before dawn to go speak somewhere, although I don't recollect now exactly where I was going. I didn't want to go. I *really* didn't want to go. For me, the glamour of travel wore off years ago. I stared at my sleep-deprived face in the mirror and wondered why I ever accepted this assignment and a hundred other assignments. As I approached the shower, I saw a note on the door which had been taped there by my wife. (See next page.)

Kim did not know this note would appear in a book one day, but notice the words: "I just want you to know how much I appreciate . . ." Clearly, Kim remembered Dr. Beckert's workshop. On the other hand, it may have had nothing to do with the workshop and it was just another evidence of my wife's gracious nature.

Look at the note again—you'll also notice the word "provide," as in "these heroic lengths you go to to provide for us." Now here's an important point— It's my *job* to provide. "The Family: A Proclamation to the World" says so. As a husband and father, it's my job to provide, preside, and protect. Kim

Good Morning Love &

I just hope you KNOW

how much I love you, &

how much I appreciate

these heroic lengths you

go to to provide for us.

Pleeeeease be careful

today! Kisses Kisses &

& Kim

should be able to *expect* this, or even *demand* it. Honey, do your job! You are supposed to provide for this family! I expect you to do your duty. However, she has never moved off *appre-ciate.*

I am the envy of thousands of men, because I have a wife who loves and appreciates me.

Well, my entire mood changed because of my wonderful wife and her simple note. She called me a hero (see line 5), she said she appreciated my work, and I could rush off to the airport looking forward to a hero's welcome upon my return.

You might also note that next to her name were lipstick prints. Those speak even louder than words. My wife loves me! She appreciates me! I am the envy of thousands of men, because I have a wife who loves and appreciates me, and she lets me know it

Her husband is the envy of thousands of men . . .
his wife appreciates him.

with notes *signed with lip prints!*

Kim knows my weaknesses better than anyone, and she could have reminded me to work on any one of them that morning. She could have pointed out my cluttered garage or my unmowed lawn. But instead she appreciated the man I was right at that moment, instead of haranguing me about the man I should be. And the net effect was that I wanted to be better for her in the future, because she loved me—as I was—right then.

I wanted to be better for her in the future, because she loved me—as I was—right then.

Hope Smiling Brightly before Us

Like most people, I watch the news and listen to the radio and feel like the world is in a downward spiral. And it is. But I have hope. President Gordon B. Hinckley had a huge impact on me. I never met him, he never called or wrote, and I never had the chance to shake his hand. But he affected my life profoundly because of his optimism. I knew from reading his biography that he was well aware of what was going on in the world. And yet, he was never "gloom and doom" as he addressed the Church and the world.

I have my worries and concerns, and you have yours. What do you say to yourself in the morning?

What pep talk do you repeat to your image in the mirror? Here's an interesting question—what about the prophet? What does he say to himself as he gets ready for the day?

> What do you say to yourself in the morning? What pep talk do you repeat to your image in the mirror?

It isn't as bad as you sometimes think it is. It all works out. Don't worry. I say that to myself every morning. It will all work out. If you do your best, it will all work out. Put your trust in God and move forward with faith and confidence in the future.[11]

—Gordon B. Hinckley

A few years ago I was working on a book, and I remembered several people reporting that Jeffrey R. Holland said something about the Savior's ultimate victory, and the "final score has already been posted," or something like that. I looked very hard for that quotation, and I just couldn't find it. Finally, I did something I had never done, and I contacted his office. His secretary told me she would try to find it. A few weeks later, I got an e-mail straight from Elder Holland that said:

From: Jeffrey R. Holland
To: John Bytheway
Subject: Quote

Oddly enough, that is something I said. It was probably at a mission conference where it was not recorded. Would you like me to restate it and authorize its use?—Jeff

I was blown away. Elder Holland was on assignment in Chile, but he took the time to e-mail me personally. Well, I responded that I would be delighted if he could restate it for me. And just before my book was about to go to press, it came. And here it is:

> The future of this world has long been declared; the final outcome between good and evil is already known. There is absolutely no question as to who wins because the victory has already been posted on the scoreboard. The only really strange thing in all of this is that we are still down here on the field trying to decide which team's jersey we want to wear![12]
>
> —Jeffrey R. Holland

Have you ever watched a replay of a football game or any athletic contest when you already knew the outcome? Have you noticed what a different experience it

> There is absolutely no question as to who wins because the victory has already been posted on the scoreboard.
>
> —Jeffrey R. Holland

Have you gotten to the part yet where they win the game?

is to watch a game when you already know what will happen?

I found a videotape of a football game from back in 2002. As I looked at the tape, I was sure the only reason I kept it was because the team I wanted to win was victorious, or I would have taped over it. So I watched the game again. And do you know what happened? My alma mater was getting *creamed.* At halftime, they were down by 27 points. And do you know what I found myself doing every time the other team scored? I laughed. I laughed! Because I knew, as improbable as it seemed, my team was going to come back and win. And they did! They squeaked by 35 to 34. The actual game must have been a real nail-biter, but watching the replay was a blast!

Well, as you watch the news, it appears we're down, and we're getting creamed. We're in the midst of a tough contest, but we're going to be okay. The Savior will be victorious, and we know it. And the downward spiral and moral decay we witness can actually *strengthen* our testimonies. "All of this is

You know whose jersey you have chosen to wear, so get off the bench and keep fighting.

supposed to happen," we can say to ourselves. You know whose jersey you have chosen to wear, so get off the bench and keep fighting. In the meantime, keep the faith. Perhaps you won't laugh when you see the world gaining yardage, but deep in your heart you can be at peace. When it appears we can't come back, you can remember the verses, "Be still, and know that I am God" (Psalm 46:10), and "If God be for us, who can be against us?" (Romans 8:31). Yeah, it's a nail-biter. But "there is hope smiling brightly before us, and we know that deliv'rance is nigh."[13]

Why Me? Why This? Why Now?

A S MY YEAR IN SEVENTH grade came to a close, my friends suggested I join them in signing up for a homemaking class. I thought they were joking. "Why do you want to take homemaking?" I asked.

"Because," they responded, "you get to eat."

That clinched the deal for me, and I signed up. The girl-to-boy ratio in the class was awesome, which was another benefit I hadn't anticipated. Anyway, almost every day in that class we made brownies. Sometimes, we overcooked them, and they were more like burnt offerings. What none of us knew was that the second half of the class was not cooking—it was sewing.

So, I learned to sew. I became adept at the Singer sewing machine. I learned how to thread the bobbin. I made a barbecuing apron that is still intact today. We also learned needlepoint. I chose an awful color of green burlap and sewed a picture of a lion's head on it. Then I gave it to my mom. What do you do with something like that? Mom hung it above her sewing machine. It was really not fit for any other room in the house, except maybe the garage.

One thing I noticed—it's important to display the right side of the fabric when doing a needlepoint. If you look at the reverse side, the criss-crossing threads make it difficult to detect what the picture is. If you framed your needlepoint wrong side out, people would ask, "What is this supposed to be?" or "What was this artist trying to portray?"

Perhaps the situation you find yourself in is not what you thought it would be. And you may wonder what the Lord is trying to do when unexpected threads weave their way through the tapestry of your life. This poem by Benjamin Malachi Franklin has blessed me and many others:

My life is but a weaving between my God and
me,
I do not choose the colors, He worketh steadily.
Ofttimes He weaveth sorrow, and I in foolish
pride,
Forget He sees the upper, and I the underside.

Not till the loom is silent, and shuttles cease to fly,
Will God unroll the canvas, and explain the
reason why.
The dark threads are as needful, in the skillful
Weaver's hand,
As the threads of gold and silver, in the pattern
He has planned.[14]

Sometimes, the answers come in this life. Most of them don't. Answers to some questions may have to wait until "the loom is silent" and our lives are

Perhaps the situation you find yourself in is not what you thought it would be. Do you wonder what the Lord is trying to do when unexpected threads weave their way through the tapestry of your life?

Our Heavenly Father doesn't usually offer explanations. If we come to understand why things happen in this life, that's a bonus. Usually, we have to wait.

over. I have concluded that our Heavenly Father doesn't usually offer explanations. If we come to understand why things happen in this life, that's a bonus. Usually, we have to wait. He just wants us to have faith in him until he comes again, when he will answer all of our questions and "reveal all things" (See D&C 101:32). In the meantime, we accept the dark threads as "needful, in the skillful weaver's hand."

Someone once said that "a blessing is anything that moves us closer to God." Trials come from a variety of places. Sometimes we cause our own problems. Sometimes things come at us that are completely out of our control. Other times another person, maybe even a loved one, misuses their agency,

My son made it, and they displayed the wrong side.
It's supposed to be a lion.

and we are hurt. In any event, like Job and Joseph and a host of others, we can always choose to move closer to God.

Perspective

I HAVE A DEAR FRIEND whom I met when I was a young college student freshly home from my mission. She taught me how to teach teenagers. Her name is Kathy Schlendorf. Kathy teaches junior high school English and French in Provo, Utah. I asked Kathy once, "Now what do you teach again?" And she said, "Manners, mostly." Kathy is a delight.

Kathy was living in Albuquerque, New Mexico, and was broadsided by a driver who wasn't paying attention. The top of her car impacted her head and peeled off much of her scalp, and her pelvis was broken in eight places, among other injuries. For seven days, the doctor told Kathy's husband that she would not make it through the night. On the eighth day, Kathy opened her eyes. She realized that she was in a hospital, and her first thought was, "That's funny, I don't remember being pregnant." She turned and saw her husband sitting there, and asked, "What happened?"

Eventually, Kathy was allowed to go home. I used to think that when they sent you home from the hospital, it meant you were all better—back to 100 percent. Then I donated a kidney, and I discovered that they release you when you are barely able to survive.

Anyway, Kathy had a little boy who, not understanding her situation, asked her to get him breakfast one day shortly after she got home. Kathy made her way, with the aid of a walker (remember, her pelvis was broken in eight places), to the cupboard. Then she realized she could not lift either hand from the walker or she would collapse. My dear friend Kathy bowed her head and began to cry as she realized her "rehab" had barely begun. Then Kathy said the Spirit spoke to her, with some fascinating words: "Kathy, you are a physical wreck." (At this point you're thinking, "Wow, that's blunt," but the Spirit wasn't finished.) "Kathy, you are a physical wreck. Now, you can either be a physical wreck *and* an emotional wreck, or you can just be a physical wreck."

Over the years, we have heard it a thousand times— we can't choose what happens to us, but we can choose how to respond to what happens to us. I'm sure that Kathy had heard it too. But in this moment, this difficult, dark, painful moment, the Spirit shed a burst of light. You can choose your response. Kathy had every right to be an emotional wreck. Her life was turned upside down by a careless driver! She was in pain! She was a physical wreck! But she

We can't choose what happens to us, but we can choose how to respond to what happens to us.

used her agency to choose her response. The way my friend Kathy, who has now had numerous "dark threads" in her life, has responded to her trials has been an inspiration to me, and perhaps to you too as I've shared her experience.

All that I've talked about in this little book can be summarized by this simple idea—*keep the Spirit of God with you.* That's it. Heber C. Kimball observed:

> I am perfectly satisfied that my Father and my God is a cheerful, pleasant, lively, and good-natured Being. Why? Because I am cheerful, pleasant, lively, and good-natured when I have His Spirit. That is one reason why I know; and another is—the Lord said, through Joseph Smith, "I delight in a glad heart and a cheerful countenance" [see D&C 59:15]. That arises from the perfection of His attributes; He is a jovial, lively person, and a beautiful man.[15]
>
> —Heber C. Kimball

Have you ever pondered the fact that God is fully aware of all the evil in the world? To a great extent, we, as human beings, can choose not to go to certain places, not to see a thousand vulgar movies, not to learn about all the unspeakable things that are going on. But God perceives them all. He is omniscient, and he knows about all the evil in this world. And yet, he is still "cheerful, pleasant, lively, and good-natured." How does he do that? I'm convinced that God doesn't mope. My respected friend and mentor, Robert L. Millet, shared this profound discovery in his book *When a Child Wanders*:

Several years ago my wife and I were struggling with how best to build faith in all of our children and how to entice wandering souls back into Church activity. A caring colleague, sensing the weight of my burdens, happened into my

> Have you ever pondered the fact that God is fully aware of all the evil in the world? He knows about all the evil in this world yet he is still "cheerful, pleasant, lively, and good-natured."

office one day and asked, "Do you think our heavenly parents wander through the heavens in morose agony over their straying children?"

Startled, I thought for a moment and said, "No, I don't think so. I know they feel pain, but I honestly can't picture them living in eternal misery."

My friend responded, "Ask yourself why they do not do so, and it will make a difference in your life." . . .

In time it began to dawn on us that the Lord knows the end from the beginning and that, as Joseph the Prophet declared, all things—past, present, and future—are and were with him "one eternal 'now'" (Smith, *Teachings of the Prophet Joseph Smith*, 220).

Perspective. PERSPECTIVE. That was the answer. God deals with pain through and by virtue of his infinite and perfect perspective. He not only knows what we have done and what we are doing, but he also knows what we will do in the future. If, as the prophets have taught, many who are heirs to the blessings of the covenant made with Abraham, Isaac, and Jacob will either in time or in eternity be reconciled to the covenant family, then all we need to do for the time being is to seek through fasting and prayer for a portion of our God's perspective—his omni-loving patience, his long-suffering, his ever-open arms, and a glimpse of the big picture. Such a perspective will not only serve us well here, in the midst of our sufferings, but it will empower our souls and fashion us into the image of our Master, who is the personification and embodiment of charity, or the pure love of Christ (see Moroni 7:45–48).[16]

—Robert L. Millet

We use the phrase "eternal perspective" so often that it's in danger of becoming a cliché. But we must never allow that to happen because an eternal perspective is the remedy for so many mortal problems. An eternal perspective makes every problem temporary, no matter how permanent it may seem right now. And access to this divine perspective is available only from God. With the Spirit of God in our lives, we feel a decrease in our competing and comparing and we grow toward contentment. The

divine promise that we can "always have his Spirit to be with [us]" makes us more delightful, and more appreciative, and although dark clouds gather, there is always hope smiling brightly before us. And while we may ask, "why me, why this, why now?" the Spirit of the Lord gives us a portion of perspective that can't be obtained from any other source, or in any other way.

I hope this little respite has recharged your batteries and prepared you to go back to the battle. Now it's time to jump back into this thing we call life. Today, you can change your part of the world. You can add a little kindness, a little caring, a little note to a friend. And when things get rough again, and you're getting fatigued and overwhelmed, remember the little things Mom

An eternal perspective makes every problem temporary, no matter how permanent it may seem right now. And access to this divine perspective is available only from God.

taught: Do your best, and learn to be content. Be good and keep the Spirit. Be nice and choose happiness when things are hard. Don't worry, God loves you, and he is near. Keep your eternal perspective. Simple? Yes. But simply true.

Notes

1. Marjorie Pay Hinckley, *Small and Simple Things* (Salt Lake City: Deseret Book, 2003), 148.
2. *Small and Simple Things,* 50.
3. Patricia Holland, "Many Things . . . One Thing" in *A Heritage of Faith: Talks Selected from the BYU Women's Conferences,* Mary E. Stovall and Carol Cornwall Madsen, eds. (Salt Lake City: Deseret Book, 1988), 15–16.
4. *Small and Simple Things,* 104.
5. http://www.xmission.com/~westra/excuseth.htm and other Internet sites; accessed 7 December 2010.
6. Wendy Watson Nelson, *Let Your Spirit Take the Lead,* audio CD (Salt Lake City: Deseret Book, 2004).

7. Jeffrey R. Holland, "Therefore, What?" An address at the 2000 New Testament Conference, Brigham Young University, 8 August 2000, 2.

8. Melvin J. Ballard, "The Sacramental Covenant," *Improvement Era,* October 1919, 1028.

9. *Small and Simple Things,* 31.

10. Katharine Hepburn, in Anne Edwards, *Katharine Hepburn: A Remarkable Woman* (New York: William Morrow and Company, 2000), 63.

11. Gordon B. Hinckley, "Messages of Inspiration from President Hinckley," *Church News,* 4 October 1997, quoted from the general session of the Jordan Utah South Regional Conference, 1 March 1997.

12. Jeffrey R. Holland, as quoted in John Bytheway, *When Times are Tough* (Salt Lake City: Deseret Book, 2004), 30.

13. "We Thank Thee, O God, for a Prophet," *Hymns of The Church of Jesus Christ of Latter-day Saints* (Salt Lake City: The Church of Jesus Christ of Latter-day Saints, 1985), no. 19.

14. Benjamin Malachi Franklin, "The Weaver," *Sourcebook of Poetry,* ed. Al Bryant (New York: Zondervan Publishing House, 1968).

15. Heber C. Kimball, in *Journal of Discourses,* vol. 4

(London: Latter-day Saints' Book Depot, 1854–1886), 222.

16. Robert L. Millet, *When a Child Wanders* (Salt Lake City: Deseret Book, 1996), 152–54.